Gettin' Around!
A Kid's Guide to Brugge, Belgium

Photography by John D. Weigand
Poetry by Penelope Dyan

Bellissima Publishing, LLC
Jamul, California
www.bellissimapublishing.com

Copyright © 2018 by Penny D. Weigand & John D. Weigand

All rights reserved. No part of this book may be
reproduced or transmitted in any form or by any means,
electronic or mechanical, including photocopying,
recording, or by any other means, or by any information or
storage retrieval system, without permission from the publisher.

ISBN 978-1-61477-331-3
First Edition

"It isn't how you get around that matters. What matters is what you see."

PENELOPE DYAN

Gettin' Around!
Bellissima Publishing, LLC

Introduction

Brugge is the capital and largest city of the province of West Flanders in the Flemish Region of Belgium. Brugge is often called the Venice of the North, because Brugge is a city with canals that are used for 'gettin' around'. It is thought that the name, Brugge more than likely came from the Old Dutch word for "bridge", which is brugga. And that makes sense, because many, many bridges go over its canal system.

There are various ways you can get around in this town; and one fun way is to travel though the pages of this book and see what our award winning author, attorney and former teacher, Penelope Dyan, and our photographer, John D. Weigand, saw as they visited Brugge. And as you travel through through the pages of this book, you can also practice your reading skills, using this 'learn to read' book filled with word repetition, and word recognition and rhyme, that has extra large print and is the perfect size for a kid's backpack!

And then when you are all finished reading, you can go to the Bellissimavideo YouTube channel and watch the free music video that goes along with this book; and you can see even more of this lovely city!

Gettin' Around!
Bellissima Publishing, LLC

Gettin' Around!
A Kid's Guide to Brugge, Belgium

Photography by John D. Weigand
Poetry by Penelope Dyan

You have arrived in Brugge!
You're in the center of town!
Mom says,
"Come on, now, let's look all around!"
You and your dad agree!
Mom says,
"Don't dawdle! We have a lot to see!"

You see horses and buggies!
Now that looks like fun!
Mom says,
"We'll do that before this day is done!"

You think out loud,
"That looks like a fun thing to do!"
But Mom says she is kind of nervous,
because no one riding those things
is anywhere nearly as young as you!

And so you walk for awhile,
and then you hop aboard a boat,
and down the canal
you roar; and you float.
You see yellow and white flowers.
You see some trees.
The boat's motor hums
like the buzzing of bees.

There are some very old buildings
that come into view.
And these very old buildings
look mysterious and creepy to you.
You wonder if a mean, old ghost
lives inside;
and so behind your dear, sweet mother
(scared) you decide to hide!

And then you see a beautiful swan!
And you feel quite all right.
Mom exclaims,
"Oh, my! What a beautiful sight!"

And then, on the shore,
you see even more!

There is a modern sculpture
that reaches up towards the sky,
It's shape reminds you
of a proud sea lion,
but you don't know exactly why.
Your mom says that art lies
in the eyes of the beholder;
and you will understand more about art,
when you are just a bit older!

And then you see a sleeping
figure on the wall by the shore,
and you wonder what else
for you lies in store.
The guide on the boat
doesn't seem impressed,
by this naked stature on the shore
that is taking a rest.

There is an outdoor market,
and Mom says,
"That looks like a fun place to shop!"
Dad smiles happily,
because the boat doesn't stop.

Then right under a bridge
your boat seems to fly,
as you marvel at the beauty
of the trees and the sky.
And as through the canal
in your boat you wend,
your mom sighs and says,
"All good things
must come to an end."
And you decide,
when the boat ride is all through,
that this boat ride
was a good and very fun thing to do!

You get off of the boat.
And you go and you buy
three chocolate frogs sweet,
that almost look too good to eat!
Behind them is a sign that says,
"Happiness is like a kiss!"
And you decide right then and there
that you'll remember this!
And you also decide that one sweet kiss
deserves another,
after you get a kiss and a frog
from your dear, sweet mother!

*"Canals, like rivers, wend through our lives.
And chocolate makes life sweet!"*

PENELOPE DYAN